zen pencils VOLUME TWO

DREAM THE IMPOSSIBLE DREAM

zen pencils VOLUME TWO

DREAM THE IMPOSSIBLE DREAM

GAVIN AUNG THAN

Andrews McMeel Publishing®

Kansas City • Sydney • London

CONTENTS

THE CALLING
BY GAVIN AUNG THAN

ENGLISH
HISTORY
SCIENCE
MATHS

SO YOU'VE DECIDED TO BE AN ARTIST.

CONGRATULATIONS.

OR SHOULD I SAY...
...COMMISERATIONS?

YOU'RE IN FOR A LIFETIME OF UNCERTAINTY.

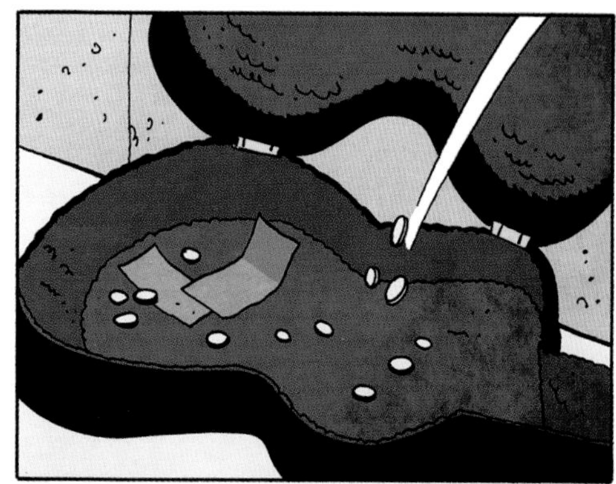

FAMILY, FRIENDS, LOVERS...

...BE PREPARED TO LOSE THEM.
KNOCK KNOCK

THIS ROAD CAN BE A LONELY ONE.

DON'T WORRY, YOU'LL MAKE NEW ACQUAINTANCES.

THEIR NAMES ARE "ANXIETY"...

..."FEAR"...

... AND "SELF-DOUBT."

THEY'LL BE BY YOUR SIDE FOREVER.

THROUGH EVERY EMBARRASSMENT...

...AND REJECTION...

...THEY ARE THERE...

...WHISPERING IN YOUR EAR...
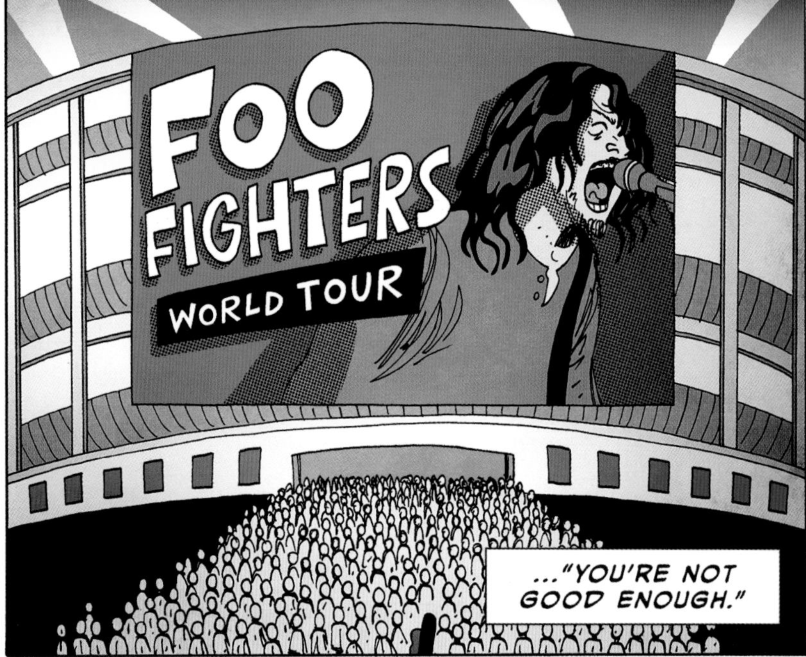
FOO FIGHTERS
WORLD TOUR
..."YOU'RE NOT GOOD ENOUGH."

YET YOU LIVE FOR *THAT* MOMENT.
WHEN THE SPARK STRIKES...

... AND YOU TOUCH THE LIGHT.

OF MY
FATE
ANGELS SING.

HEAVENS PART.

THE ROK
ROK
NEW GENESIS
the last band on earth
LIVE MUSIC

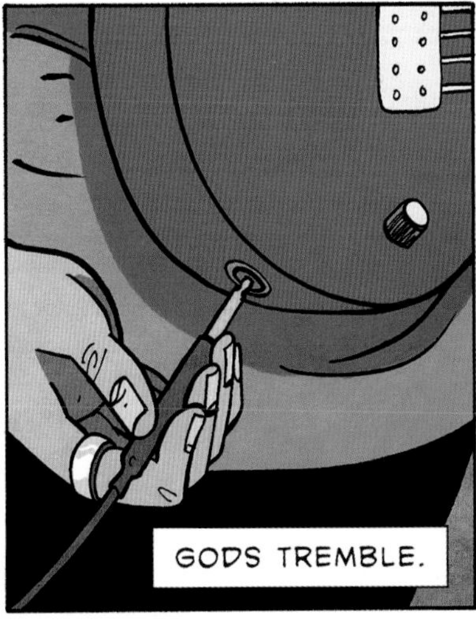
GODS TREMBLE.

CREATIVITY!

NEW GENESIS

THE SACRIFICE REPAID IN FULL.

♫
12B
12A

AT LEAST THAT'S WHAT YOU TELL YOURSELF.

12B
EVICTION NOTICE
TWO STEPS FORWARD, ONE STEP BACK...

...ON A JOURNEY
THAT NEVER ENDS.
DING
DONG

YAWN

BUT DON'T LET ME
SCARE YOU.

THE DECISION WAS NEVER YOURS TO MAKE.

AFTER ALL, YOU DON'T CHOOSE YOUR CALLING.

THE CALLING CHOOSES YOU.

ISAAC ASIMOV

A LIFETIME OF LEARNING

COMMUNITY CENTR
ADULT COURSES
NOW YOU'RE AN ADULT.

YOU DON'T DO THAT SORT OF THING ANYMORE.
LANDSCAPE PAINTING FOR BEGINNERS 6.30-8.30PM

YOU HAVE EVERYBODY LOOKING FORWARD TO NO LONGER LEARNING...
COMPOSITION
- RULE OF THIRDS
- SYMMETRICAL vs ASYMMETRICAL

...AND YOU MAKE THEM ASHAMED AFTERWARD OF GOING BACK TO LEARNING.

IF YOU HAVE A SYSTEM OF EDUCATION USING COMPUTERS...
Princetown College
Certified public accountant

...THEN ANYONE, ANY AGE, CAN LEARN BY THEMSELVES AND CAN CONTINUE TO BE INTERESTED.
YouToob
dscape painting TUTORIAL p1

IF YOU ENJOY LEARNING...

PARIS
PARIS
FRANCE
TRAVEL GUIDE
FRANCE

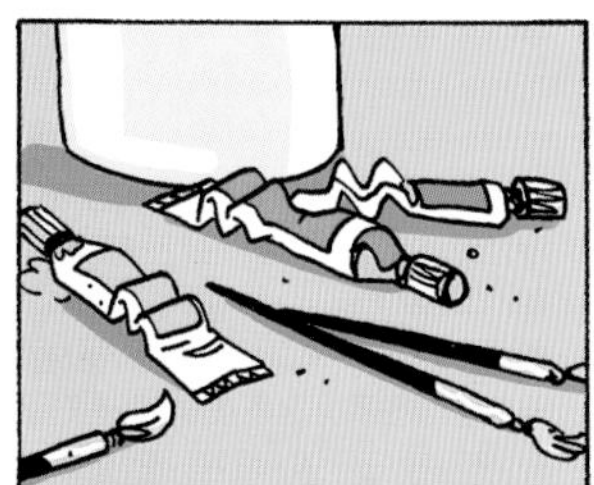

LEARN FRENCH
LESSON ONE

...THERE'S NO REASON WHY YOU SHOULD STOP AT A GIVEN AGE.
BONJOUR
BONJOUR

IT SEEMS TO ME...

...THAT WHEN IT'S TIME TO DIE...
...AND THAT WILL COME TO ALL OF US...

...THERE WOULD BE A CERTAIN PLEASURE IN THINKING THAT YOU HAD UTILIZED YOUR LIFE WELL...

...THAT YOU HAD LEARNED AS MUCH AS YOU COULD...
こんにちは
こんにちは
JAPAN GUIDE
JAPAN

食
KIRIN
プロミス
SUSHI
ラーメン
...GATHERED IN AS MUCH AS POSSIBLE OF THE UNIVERSE...

... AND ENJOYED IT.

THERE'S ONLY THIS ONE UNIVERSE AND ONLY THIS ONE LIFETIME TO TRY TO GRASP IT.

おはようございます,
お元気ですか?
わたしは元気です,
ありがとう.

AND WHILE IT IS INCONCEIVABLE THAT ANYONE CAN GRASP MORE THAN A TINY PORTION OF IT...

...THEY CAN AT LEAST DO THAT MUCH.

WHAT A TRAGEDY JUST TO PASS THROUGH AND GET NOTHING OUT OF IT.
- ISAAC ASIMOV

THE GIFT OF LIFE

CHRIS HARDWICK

YOU ARE THE PROPRIETOR OF YOUR THOUGHTS AND FEELINGS...

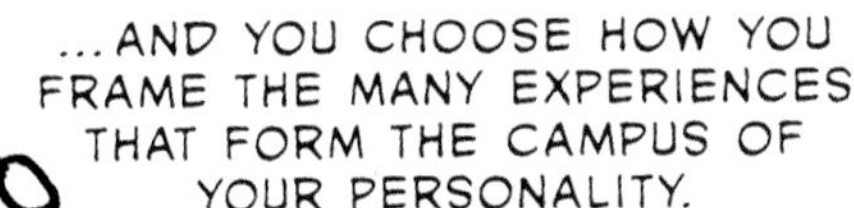
...AND YOU CHOOSE HOW YOU FRAME THE MANY EXPERIENCES THAT FORM THE CAMPUS OF YOUR PERSONALITY.

SMASH!

!
SQUEEEEEEEEEEEEE

IT'S A WEIRD AND GLORIOUS MOMENT OF SELF-AWARENESS...
...THE DAY YOU REALIZE THAT YOU ARE THE WARDEN...

...RATHER THAN THE PRISONER OF YOUR EMOTIONS.
POOF!
CLICK!

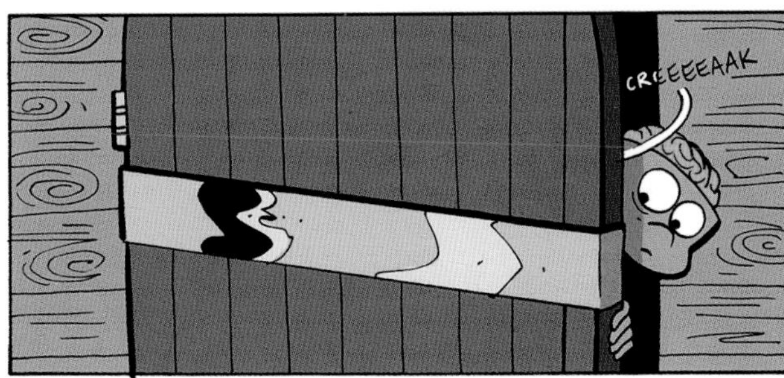
CREEEEAAK

THE INTERESTING THING ABOUT OUR MINDS...

...THEY DEFAULT
TO ***AUTOPILOT***.

SMASH
SMASH

! ! ! ! ! ! !

POF
CLICK!

SWISH!

...FLOATING THROUGH THE UNIVERSE LIKE A GHOST SHIP...

... MERELY REACTING
TO WHEREVER IT TAKES YOU.

AWESOMELY, YOU DON'T HAVE TO GO ALONG WITH IT.
– CHRIS HARDWICK

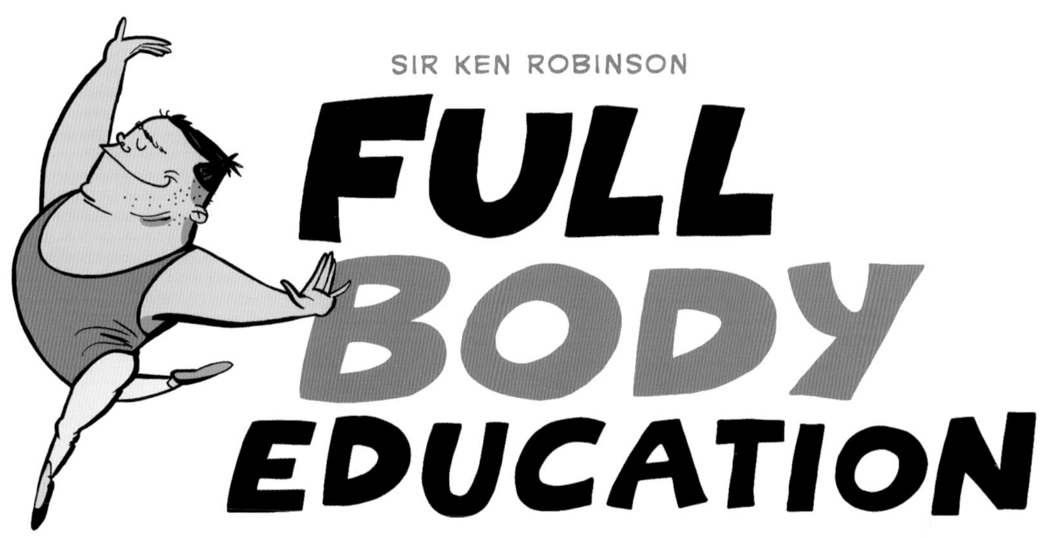
SIR KEN ROBINSON
FULL
BODY
EDUCATION

EVERY EDUCATION SYSTEM ON EARTH HAS THE SAME HIERARCHY OF SUBJECTS.

EVERY ONE.

DOESN'T MATTER WHERE YOU GO.
ROBINSON
PUBLIC SCHOOL
YOU'D THINK IT WOULD BE OTHERWISE, BUT IT ISN'T.

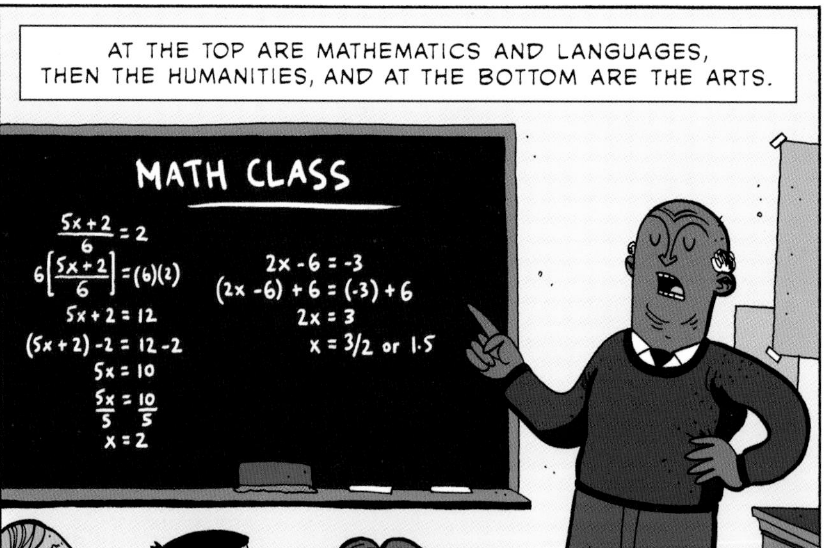
AT THE TOP ARE MATHEMATICS AND LANGUAGES, THEN THE HUMANITIES, AND AT THE BOTTOM ARE THE ARTS.
MATH CLASS
5x + 2 / 6 = 2
6[5x + 2 / 6] = (6)(2)
5x + 2 = 12
(5x + 2) - 2 = 12 - 2
5x = 10
5x / 5 = 10 / 5
x = 2
2x - 6 = -3
(2x - 6) + 6 = (-3) + 6
2x = 3
x = 3/2 or 1.5

EVERYWHERE ON EARTH.

ALGEBRA EXAM
F

RING RING
RING RING

ROOM 2C

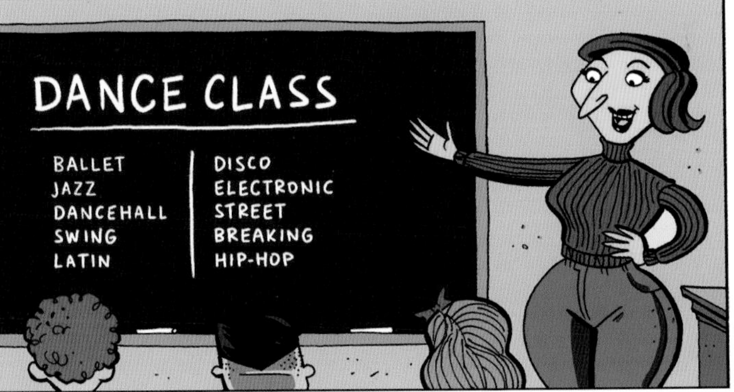

WHY NOT? I THINK THIS IS RATHER IMPORTANT.

...BUT SO IS DANCE.

CHILDREN DANCE ALL THE TIME IF THEY'RE ALLOWED TO.
WE ALL DO.

WE ALL HAVE BODIES,
DON'T WE?

DID I MISS A
MEETING?
HIGH PRIORITY
MATH
SCIENCE
LANGUAGES
HUMANITIES
LOW PRIORITY
ART
MUSIC
DANCE
BOARD OF EDUCATION

TRUTHFULLY, WHAT HAPPENS IS, AS CHILDREN GROW UP, WE START TO EDUCATE THEM PROGRESSIVELY FROM THE WAIST UP.
EDUCATION GUIDELINES OF 1892
AND THEN WE FOCUS ON THEIR HEADS...

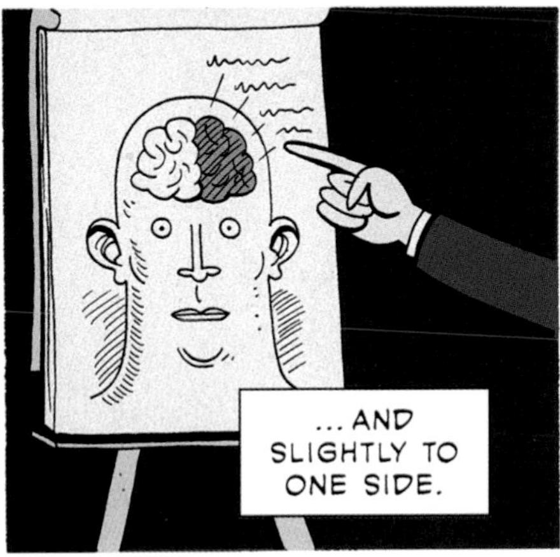
...AND SLIGHTLY TO ONE SIDE.

OUR EDUCATION SYSTEM IS PREDICATED ON THE IDEA OF ACADEMIC ABILITY.
LEFT BRAIN
ANALYTIC THOUGHT
LANGUAGE
LOGIC
SCIENCE & MATH

AND THERE'S A REASON.
BOARD OF EDUCAT

THE WHOLE SYSTEM WAS INVENTED TO MEET THE NEEDS OF INDUSTRIALISM.

SO YOU WERE PROBABLY STEERED BENIGNLY AWAY FROM THINGS AT SCHOOL WHEN YOU WERE A KID.
WELCOME TO PARENT TEACHER NIGHT
PRINCIPAL

THINGS YOU LIKED.

ON THE GROUNDS THAT YOU WOULD **NEVER** GET A JOB DOING THAT.

DON'T DO MUSIC, YOU'RE NOT GOING TO BE A MUSICIAN. ***DON'T*** DO ART, YOU WON'T BE AN ARTIST.
ROYAL ACADEMY OF DANCE
Scholarship application

AND FOR THE FUTURE, IT WON'T SERVE US.

ROYAL BALLET PRESENTS

The Nutcracker

"Spellbinding."

"Magical."

WE HAVE TO RETHINK THE FUNDAMENTAL PRINCIPLES ON WHICH WE'RE EDUCATING OUR CHILDREN.

– SIR KEN ROBINSON

KEVIN SMITH

IT COSTS NOTHING TO ENCOURAGE AN ARTIST

REMEMBER...

...IT COSTS NOTHING TO ENCOURAGE AN ARTIST.

AND THE POTENTIAL BENEFITS ARE STAGGERING.
SCRIBBLE SCRIBBLE

SCRIBBLE SCRIBBLE

CALARTS
ANIMATION DEPARTME

DISNEE
STUDIOS

DISNEE ANIMATION PRESENTS

THE DINOMITES

COMING SOON

VARIETY
DINOS DOMINATE BOX OFFICE
BIGGEST OPENING WEEKEND EVER
DINOMITES
SESSIONS ADDED
THE DINOMITES
EXTRA SESSIONS ADDED
BOX OFFICE

A PAT ON THE BACK TO AN ARTIST NOW...
OMITES
UT NOW ON
U-RAY + DVD

...COULD ONE DAY RESULT IN YOUR FAVORITE FILM...

...OR THE CARTOON YOU LOVE TO GET STONED WATCHING...

Katy Ferry - Dino Roar
KatyFerryOfficial
Subscribe

...OR THE SONG THAT SAVES YOUR LIFE.

$24.95
$24.95

WINNER
The Dinomites
Best Animated Feature

THANKSGIVING
DAY
PARADE

DISCOURAGE AN ARTIST...
THE
DINOMITES

...YOU GET ABSOLUTELY NOTHING IN RETURN, EVER.
-KEVIN SMITH
SCRUNCH!

AMY POEHLER

GREAT PEOPLE DO THINGS BEFORE THEY'RE READY

THEY DO THINGS BEFORE THEY KNOW THEY CAN DO IT.

DOING WHAT YOU'RE AFRAID OF, GETTING OUT OF YOUR COMFORT ZONE, TAKING RISKS LIKE THAT...
... THAT'S WHAT LIFE IS.

YOU MIGHT BE REALLY GOOD.
YOU MIGHT FIND OUT SOMETHING ABOUT
YOURSELF THAT'S REALLY SPECIAL.
AND IF
YOU'RE NOT
GOOD...

YOU TRIED SOMETHING.

YOUTH
RECREATION
CENTRE

COMEDY
CLASSES
·ACTING·
·STAND-UP·
·IMPROV·

NOW YOU
KNOW SOMETHING
ABOUT YOURSELF.
-AMY POEHLER

ALBERT CAMUS
THE MIDDLE OF WINTER
A love story: PART ONE

I DISCOVERED ONCE MORE AT TIPASA THAT ONE MUST KEEP INTACT IN ONESELF A FRESHNESS, A COOL WELL-SPRING OF JOY, LOVE THE DAY THAT ESCAPES INJUSTICE, AND RETURN TO COMBAT HAVING WON THAT LIGHT.

HERE I RECAPTURED THE OLD BEAUTY, A YOUNG SKY...

...AND I MEASURED MY LUCK...

...REALIZING AT LAST...
...THAT IN THE WORST YEARS OF OUR MADNESS...

...THE MEMORY OF THAT SKY HAD NEVER LEFT ME.

THIS WAS WHAT IN THE END HAD KEPT ME FROM DESPAIRING.

THERE THE WORLD BEGAN OVER AGAIN EVERY DAY IN AN EVER NEW LIGHT.

O LIGHT!

THIS IS THE CRY OF ALL THE CHARACTERS OF ANCIENT DRAMA BROUGHT FACE TO FACE WITH THEIR FATE.

THIS LAST RESORT WAS OURS, TOO...

...AND I KNEW IT NOW.

... AN INVINCIBLE SUMMER.

-ALBERT CAMUS

A love story:
PART TWO

IF YOU LOVE SOMEONE...

BLAH
BLAH
BLAH
BLAH BLAH
BLAH
BLAH

CUPID
ONLINE DATING
APPLY

GULP

SNAP!

BLAH BLAH BLAH BLAH BLAH BLAH BLAH BLAH BLAH BLAH BLAH BLAH BLAH

IF THEY
COME
BACK...

... THEY'RE YOURS.
-AUTHOR UNKNOWN

BECAUSE IT'S THERE

GEORGE MALLORY

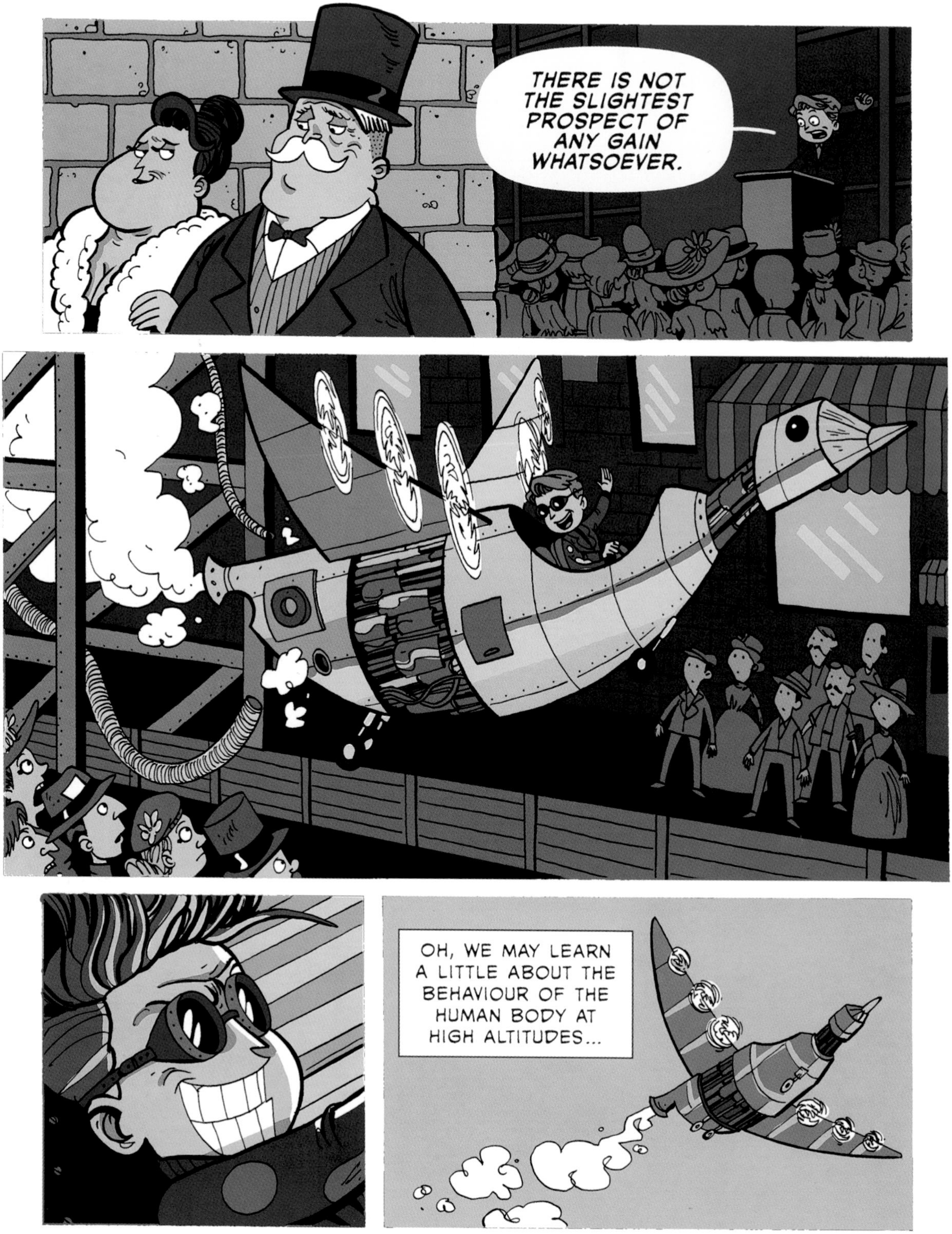

THERE IS NOT THE SLIGHTEST PROSPECT OF ANY GAIN WHATSOEVER.

OH, WE MAY LEARN A LITTLE ABOUT THE BEHAVIOUR OF THE HUMAN BODY AT HIGH ALTITUDES...

...AND POSSIBLY MEDICAL MEN MAY TURN OUR OBSERVATION TO SOME ACCOUNT FOR THE PURPOSES OF AVIATION.

NOT A GEM, NOR
ANY COAL OR IRON.

IF YOU CANNOT UNDERSTAND
THAT THERE IS SOMETHING IN
MAN WHICH RESPONDS TO THE
CHALLENGE OF THIS MOUNTAIN...

...AND
GOES OUT TO
MEET IT...

...THAT THE STRUGGLE
IS THE STRUGGLE OF
LIFE ITSELF...

...UPWARD AND
FOREVER UPWARD...

...THEN YOU WON'T SEE WHY WE GO.

WHAT WE GET FROM
THIS ADVENTURE IS
JUST SHEER *JOY*.

AND JOY IS, AFTER ALL...

...THE END
OF LIFE.

WE DO NOT LIVE TO EAT
AND MAKE MONEY.

PUT PUT PUT
PUT PUT

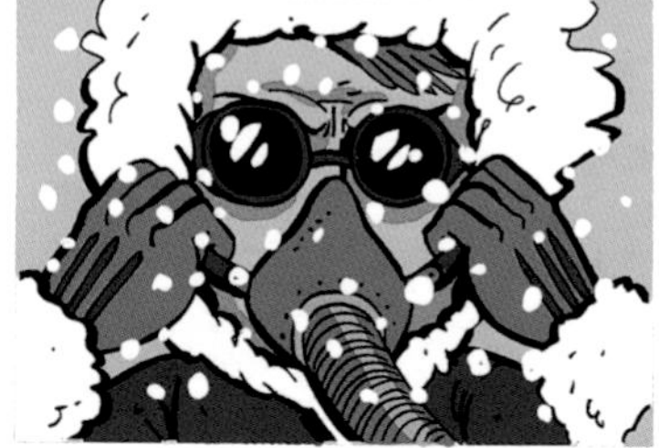

WE EAT AND MAKE MONEY TO BE ABLE TO *LIVE.*
PUT PUT PUT PUT PUT PUT PUT PUT

PUT PUT PUT PUT PUT PUT PUT PUT PUT PUT PUT PUT

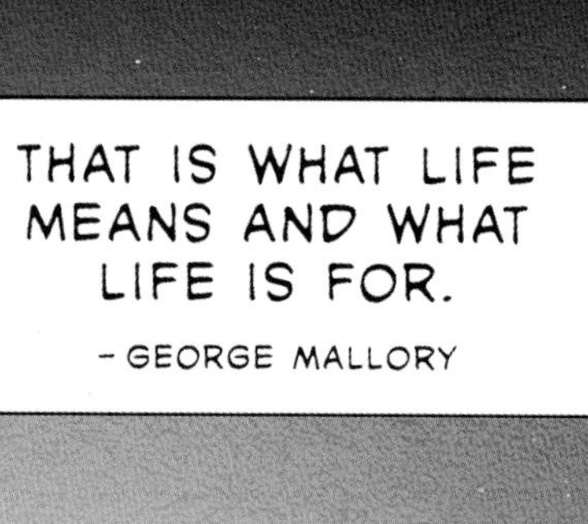
THAT IS WHAT LIFE MEANS AND WHAT LIFE IS FOR.
- GEORGE MALLORY

THE DALAI LAMA

WE ARE ALL HUMAN BEINGS

DANGER! BEWARE!
WATCHTOWER PROTECTED

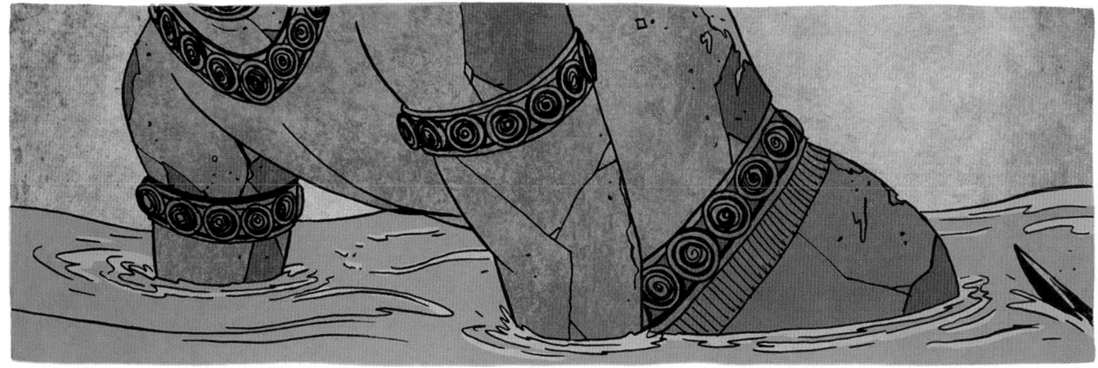

... I AM ALWAYS
REMINDED THAT
WE ARE ALL
BASICALLY ALIKE.

WE ARE ALL
HUMAN BEINGS.

MAYBE WE
HAVE DIFFERENT
CLOTHES...

...OUR
SKIN IS OF A
DIFFERENT
COLOUR...

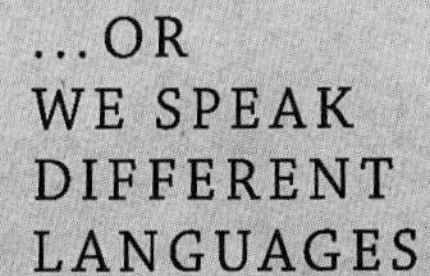
...OR
WE SPEAK
DIFFERENT
LANGUAGES.

THAT IS ON THE SURFACE.

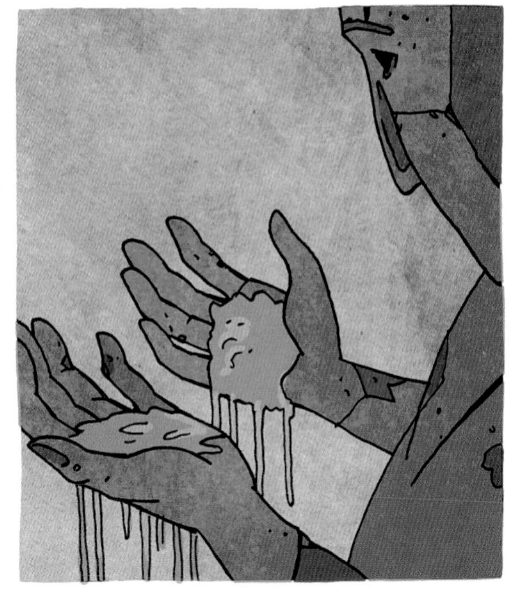

BUT BASICALLY, WE ARE THE SAME HUMAN BEINGS.

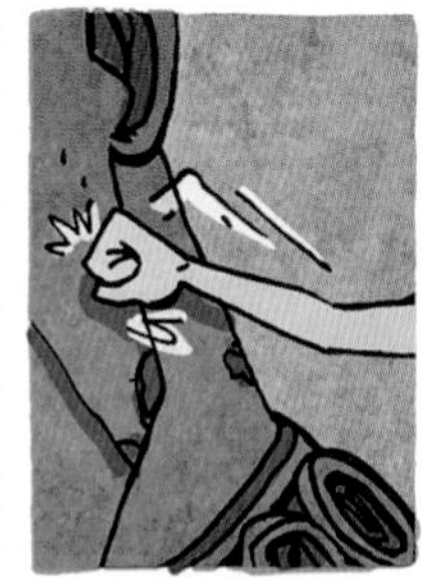

THAT IS WHAT BINDS US TO EACH OTHER.

THAT IS WHAT MAKES IT POSSIBLE FOR US TO UNDERSTAND EACH OTHER...

... AND TO DEVELOP FRIENDSHIP AND CLOSENESS.

– TENZIN GYATSO, 14TH DALAI LAMA

The fears are paper tigers

AMELIA EARHART

MONSTER!

MONSTER!

SWIPE!

THE MOST DIFFICULT THING IS THE DECISION TO ACT.

THE REST
IS MERELY
TENACITY.

SQUISH
SQUISH

THE FEARS ARE PAPER TIGERS.

YOU CAN ACT TO CHANGE AND CONTROL YOUR LIFE...
...AND THE PROCEDURE, THE PROCESS IS ITS OWN REWARD.
-AMELIA EARHART

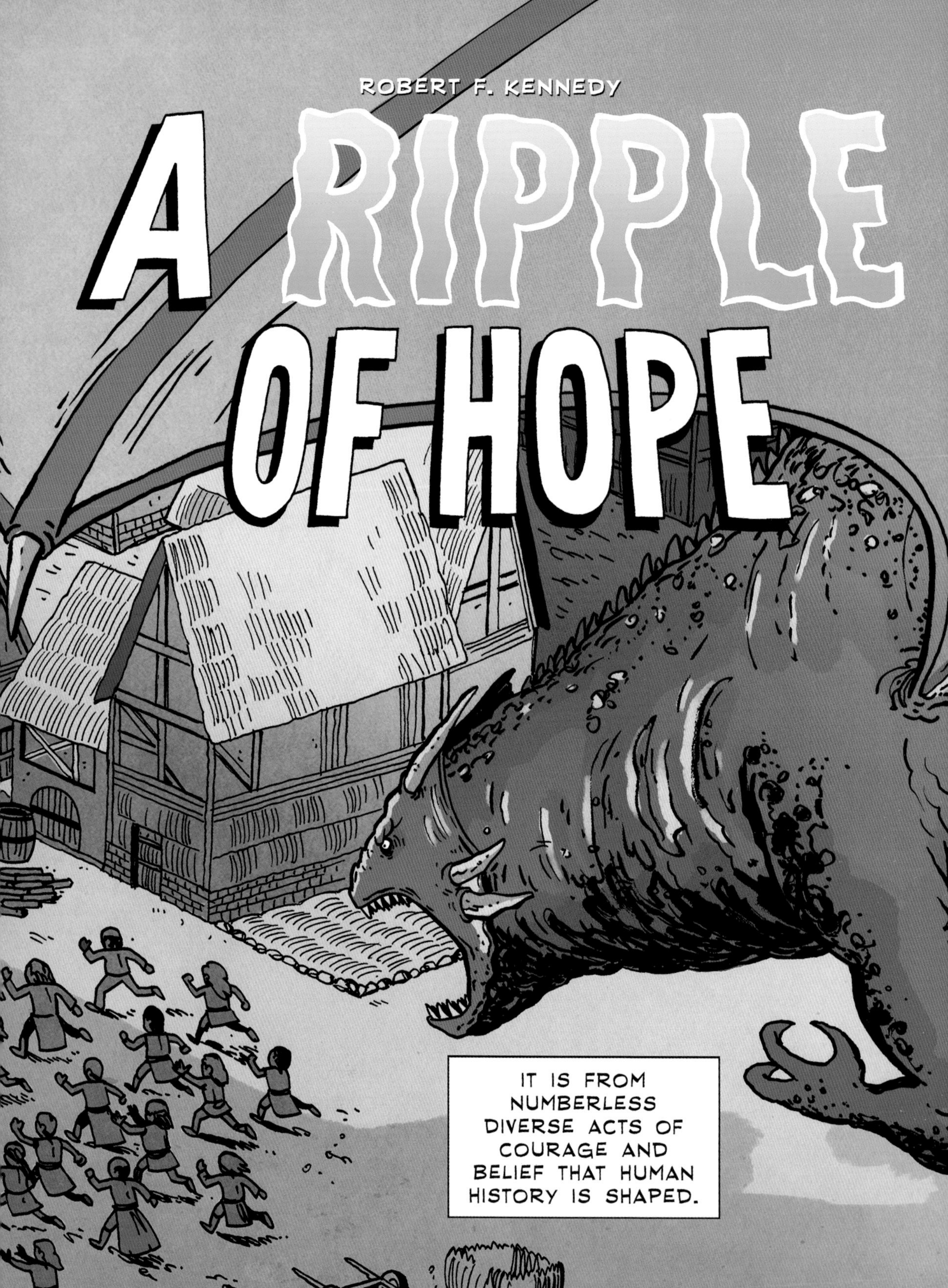
ROBERT F. KENNEDY
A RIPPLE OF HOPE
IT IS FROM NUMBERLESS DIVERSE ACTS OF COURAGE AND BELIEF THAT HUMAN HISTORY IS SHAPED.

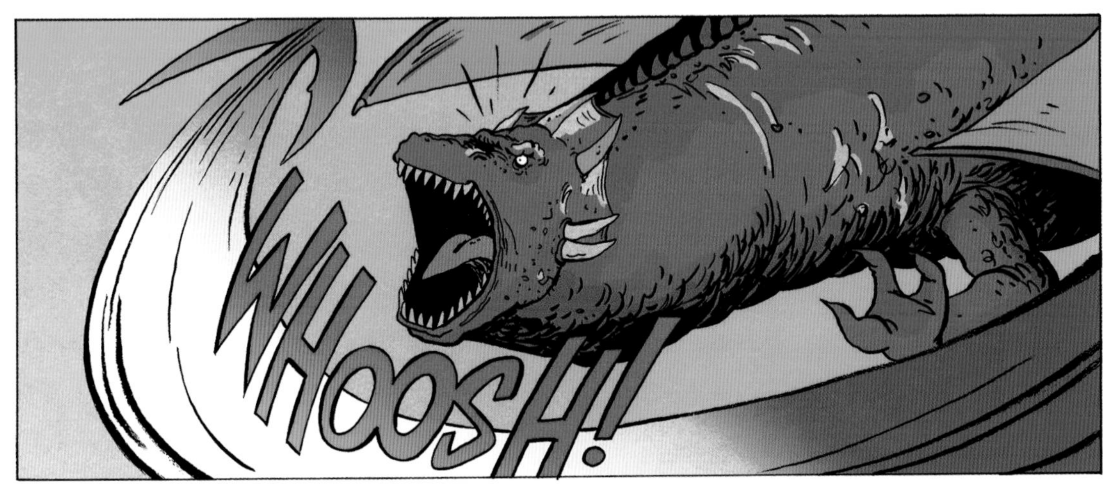
WHOOSH!

EACH TIME A MAN STANDS UP FOR AN IDEAL...

...OR ACTS TO IMPROVE THE LOT OF OTHERS...

...OR STRIKES
OUT AGAINST INJUSTICE...

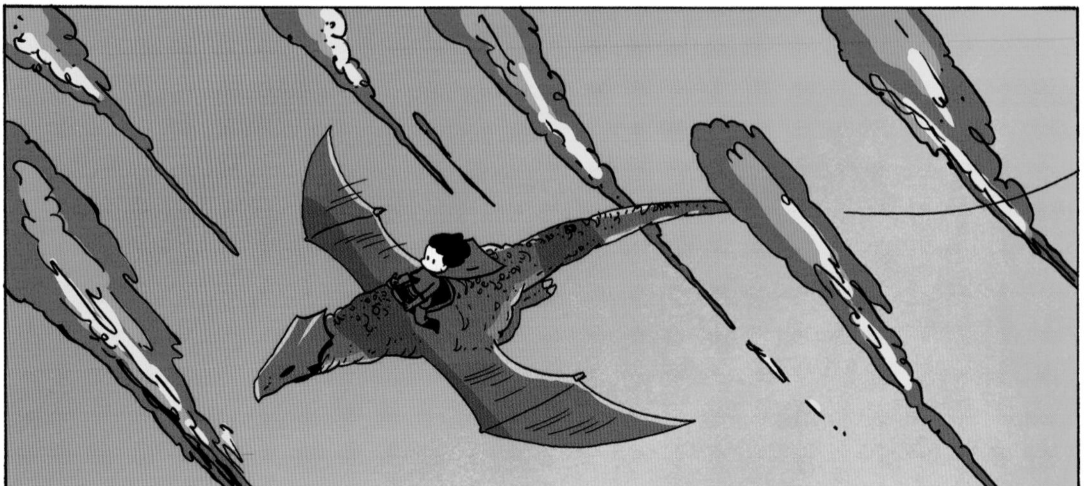

WHACK!

...HE SENDS FORTH A TINY RIPPLE OF HOPE.

AND CROSSING EACH OTHER FROM A MILLION DIFFERENT CENTERS OF ENERGY AND DARING...

...THOSE
RIPPLES BUILD
A CURRENT...

...WHICH CAN SWEEP DOWN
THE MIGHTIEST WALLS OF
OPPRESSION AND RESISTANCE.
- ROBERT F. KENNEDY

IT COULDN'T BE DONE

A POEM BY

EDGAR ALBERT GUEST

RUN 4 CHARITY
MARATHON
HALF FULL REGISTER

REGIS
CLICK!

...WHO WOULDN'T SAY SO TILL HE'D TRIED.

SO HE BUCKLED RIGHT IN...

...WITH THE TRACE OF A GRIN ON HIS FACE.

IF HE WORRIED HE HID IT.

EYE OF THE TIGER
HE STARTED TO SING...

...AS HE TACKLED THE THING...

...THAT COULDN'T BE DONE...

...AND HE DID IT!

Krispy Kreme
Krispy Kreme
Krispy Kreme
Krispy Kreme
PEANUT BUTTER
PEANUT BUTTER
OREO
OREO
OREO
Chip
Chips
SOMEBODY SCOFFED...
TimTam
TimTam
OH, YOU'LL NEVER DO THAT.
Cheetos
Cheeto

AT LEAST NO ONE EVER HAS DONE IT.

BUT HE TOOK OFF HIS COAT AND HE TOOK OFF HIS HAT...

...AND THE FIRST THING WE KNEW HE'D BEGUN IT.

YEARLY PLANNER
HE STARTED TO SING...
♫
GOJI BERRIES
BIG DIET BOOK

... AS HE TACKLED THE THING...

... THAT COULDN'T BE DONE...
GULP!

... AND HE DID IT.

THERE ARE THOUSANDS TO TELL YOU IT CANNOT BE DONE.

THERE ARE THOUSANDS TO PROPHESY FAILURE.
STAIRS

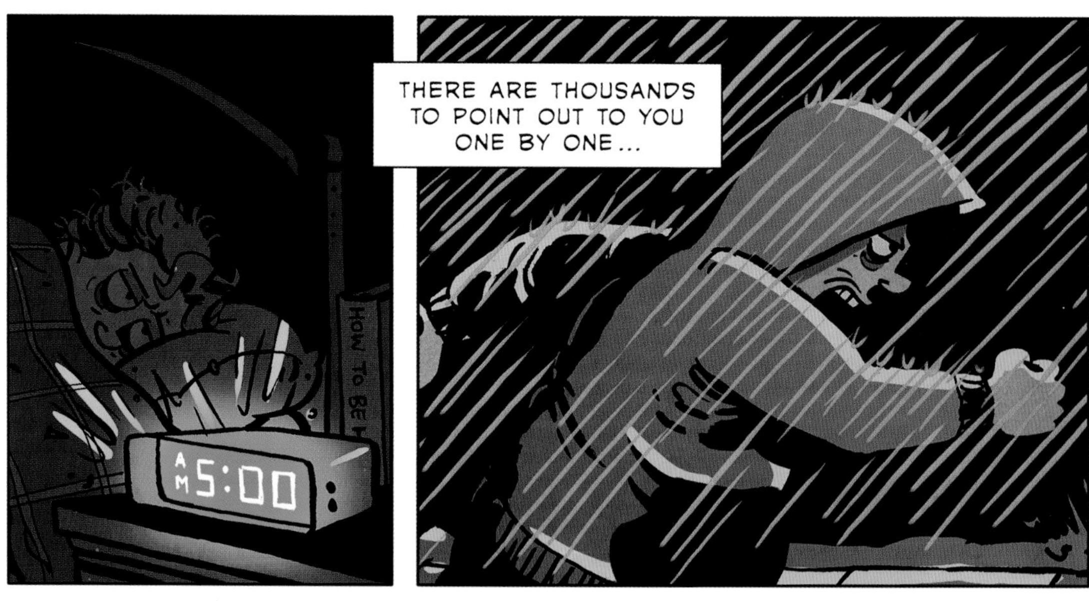
HOW TO BE
AM 5:00
THERE ARE THOUSANDS TO POINT OUT TO YOU ONE BY ONE...

...THE DANGERS THAT WAIT TO ASSAIL YOU.

BUT JUST BUCKLE IN WITH A BIT OF A GRIN.

JUST TAKE OFF YOUR COAT...

...AND GO TO IT.

JUST START IN TO SING AS YOU TACKLE THE THING...

THAT "CANNOT BE DONE"...
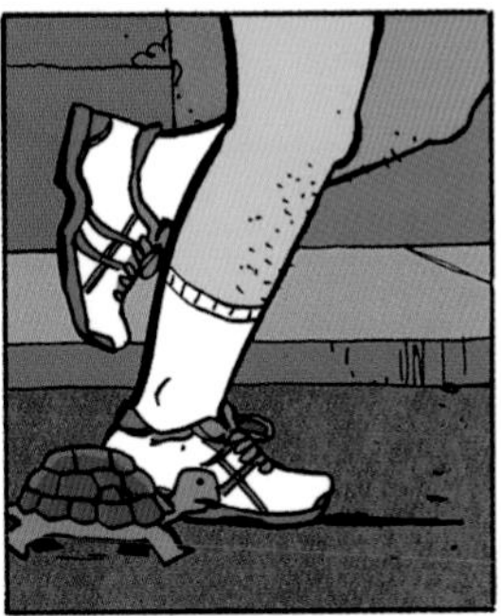

FINISH
... AND YOU'LL DO IT.
– EDGAR ALBERT GUEST

I met a traveller from an antique land who said...

Two vast and trunkless legs of stone stand in the desert.

...half sunk, a shattered visage lies.
Whose frown,
and wrinkled lip...

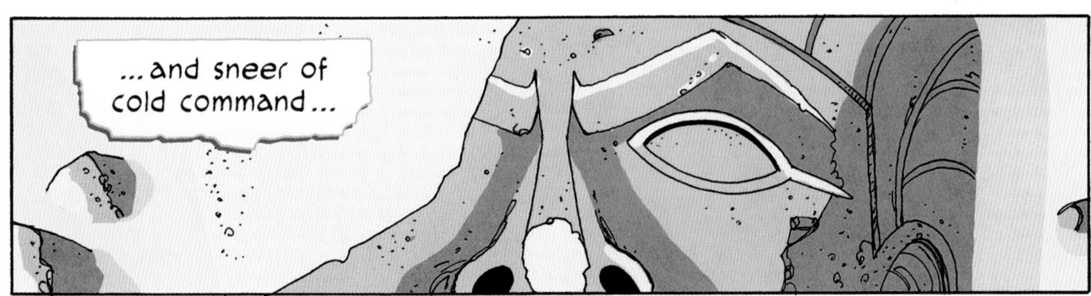
...and sneer of
cold command...

...tell that its
sculptor well those
passions read.

Which yet survive, stamped on these lifeless things.

The hand that mocked them...

...and the heart that fed.

And on the pedestal these words appear...

MY NAME IS OZYMANDIAS.

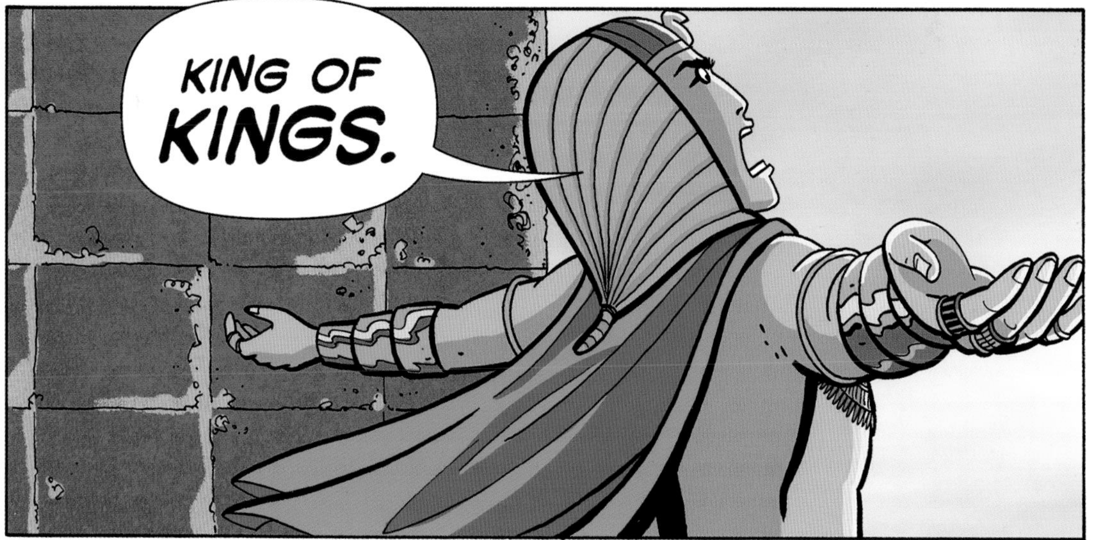
KING OF KINGS.

LOOK ON MY WORKS, YE MIGHTY...
...AND DESPAIR!

Nothing beside remains.

...boundless and bare...

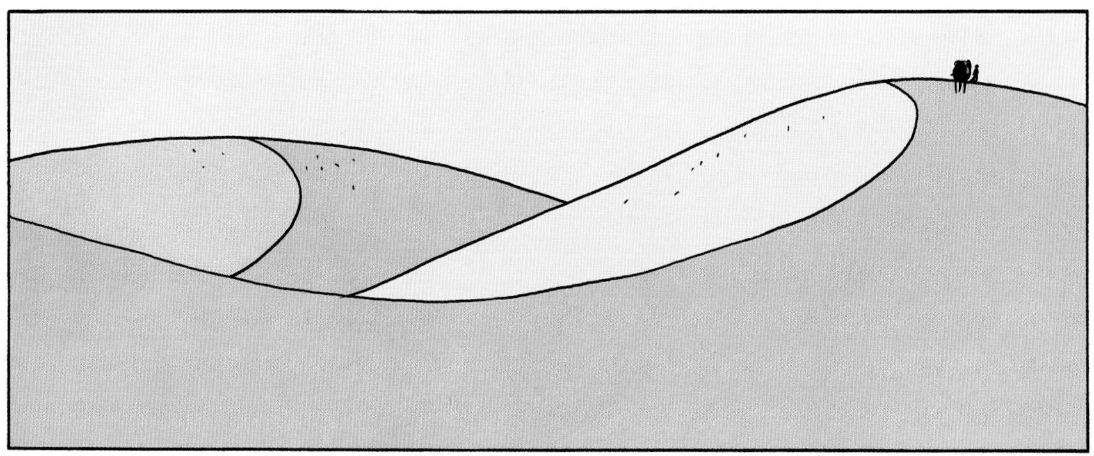

...the lone and level sands stretch far away.
- Percy Bysshe Shelley

PHENOMENAL WOMAN

A POEM BY ***MAYA ANGELOU***

PRETTY WOMEN
WONDER

WHERE MY
SECRET LIES.

I SAY...
IT'S IN THE REACH OF MY ARMS
NO COLORED

THE SPAN OF MY HIPS
CANDY

THE STRIDE OF MY STEP

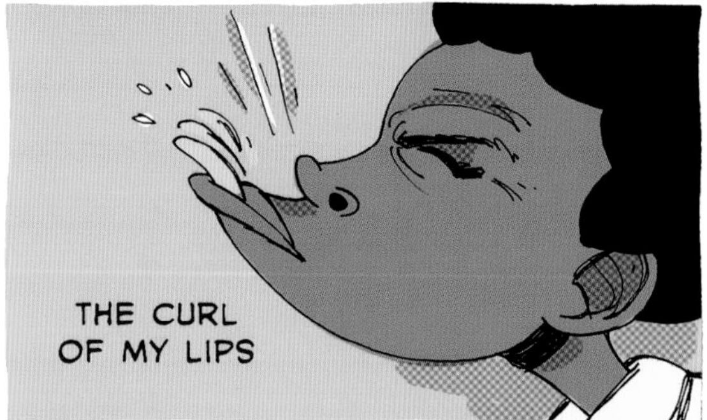
THE CURL OF MY LIPS

I'M A WOMAN
PHENOMENALLY.

PHENOMENAL WOMAN

THAT'S ME.

I WALK INTO A ROOM

JUST AS COOL AS YOU PLEASE

AND TO A MAN, THE FELLOWS STAND OR...
...FALL DOWN ON THEIR KNEES.

THEN THEY SWARM AROUND ME, A HIVE OF HONEY BEES.
I SAY...
IT'S THE FIRE IN MY EYES

AND THE FLASH OF MY TEETH

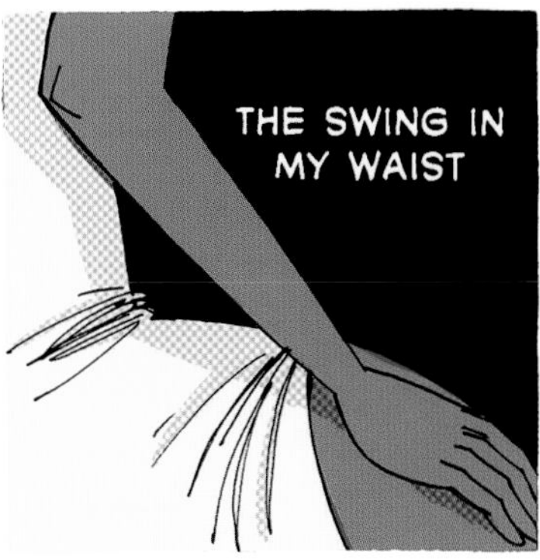
THE SWING IN MY WAIST

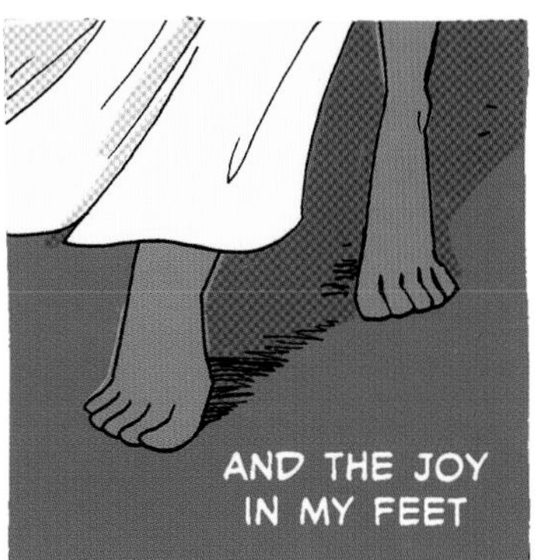
AND THE JOY IN MY FEET

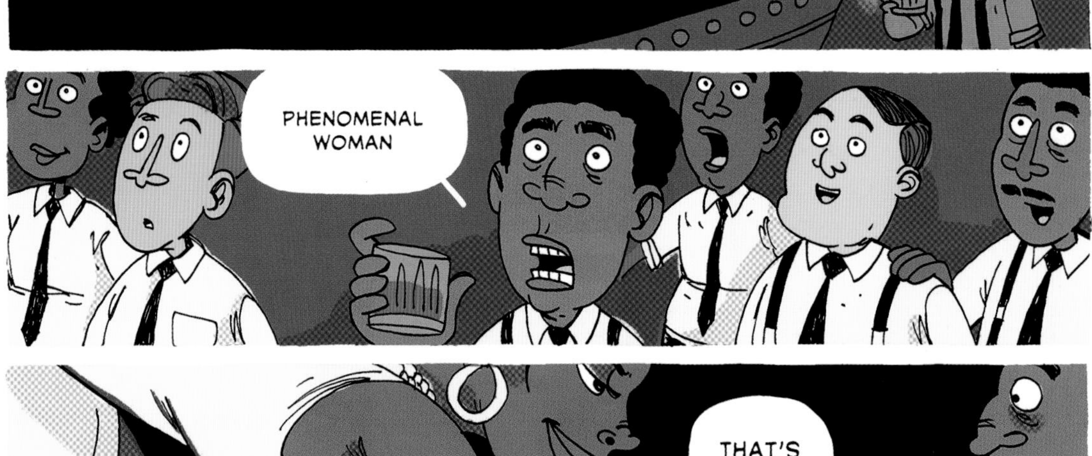
I'M A WOMAN
PHENOMENALLY.
PHENOMENAL WOMAN
THAT'S ME.

MEN THEMSELVES
HAVE WONDERED
WHAT THEY SEE IN ME.

THEY TRY
SO MUCH
BUT THEY
CAN'T
TOUCH ...
NAACP
BENEFIT

... MY INNER
MYSTERY.

WHEN I TRY TO SHOW THEM ...
... THEY SAY THEY
STILL CAN'T SEE.
CLAP
CLAP
CLAP
CLAP
CLAP CLAP
CLAP
CLAP

I'M A WOMAN PHENOMENALLY.

PHENOMENAL WOMAN

THAT'S ME.

Now You Understand...

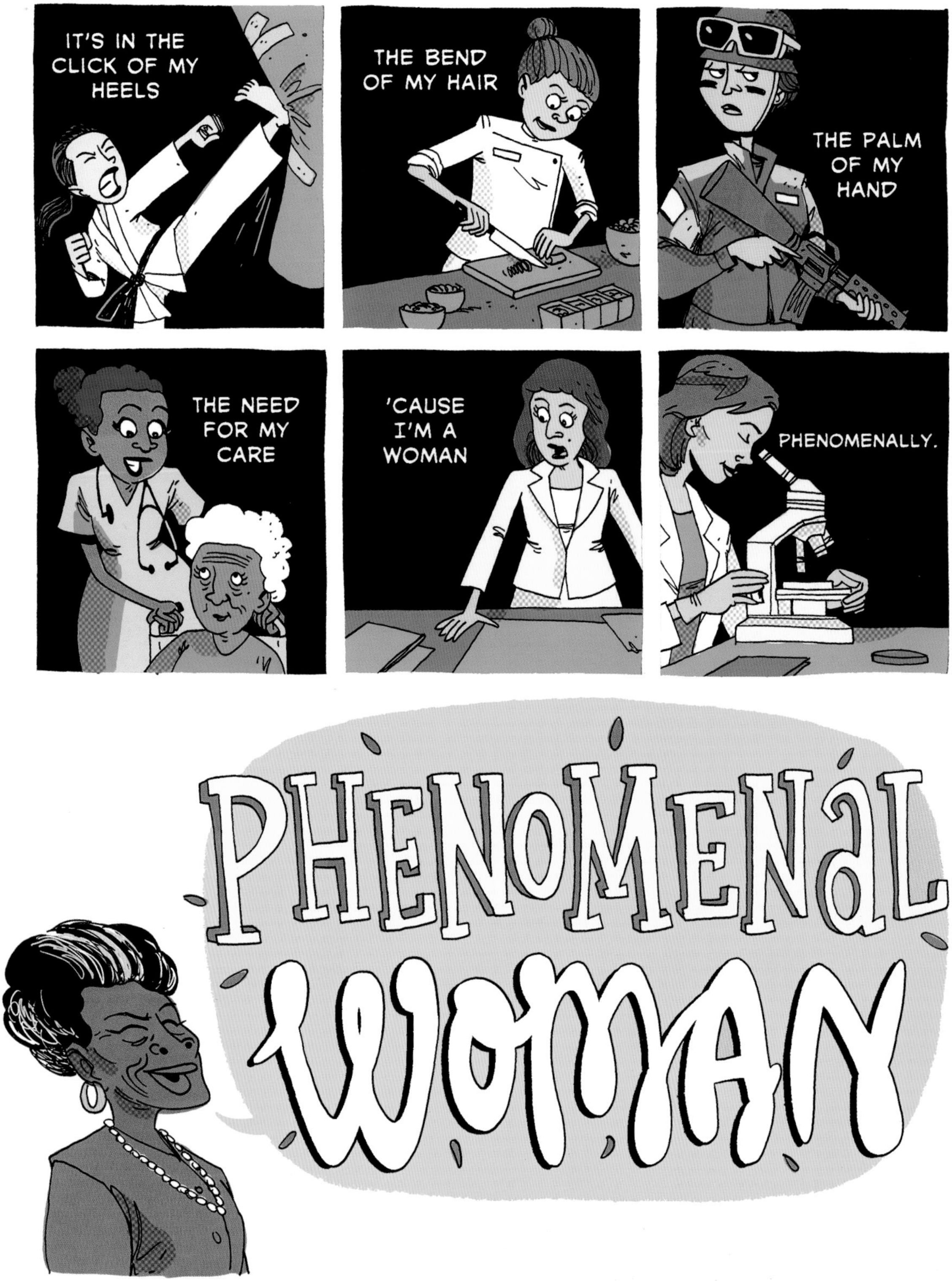

PHENOMENAL WOMAN

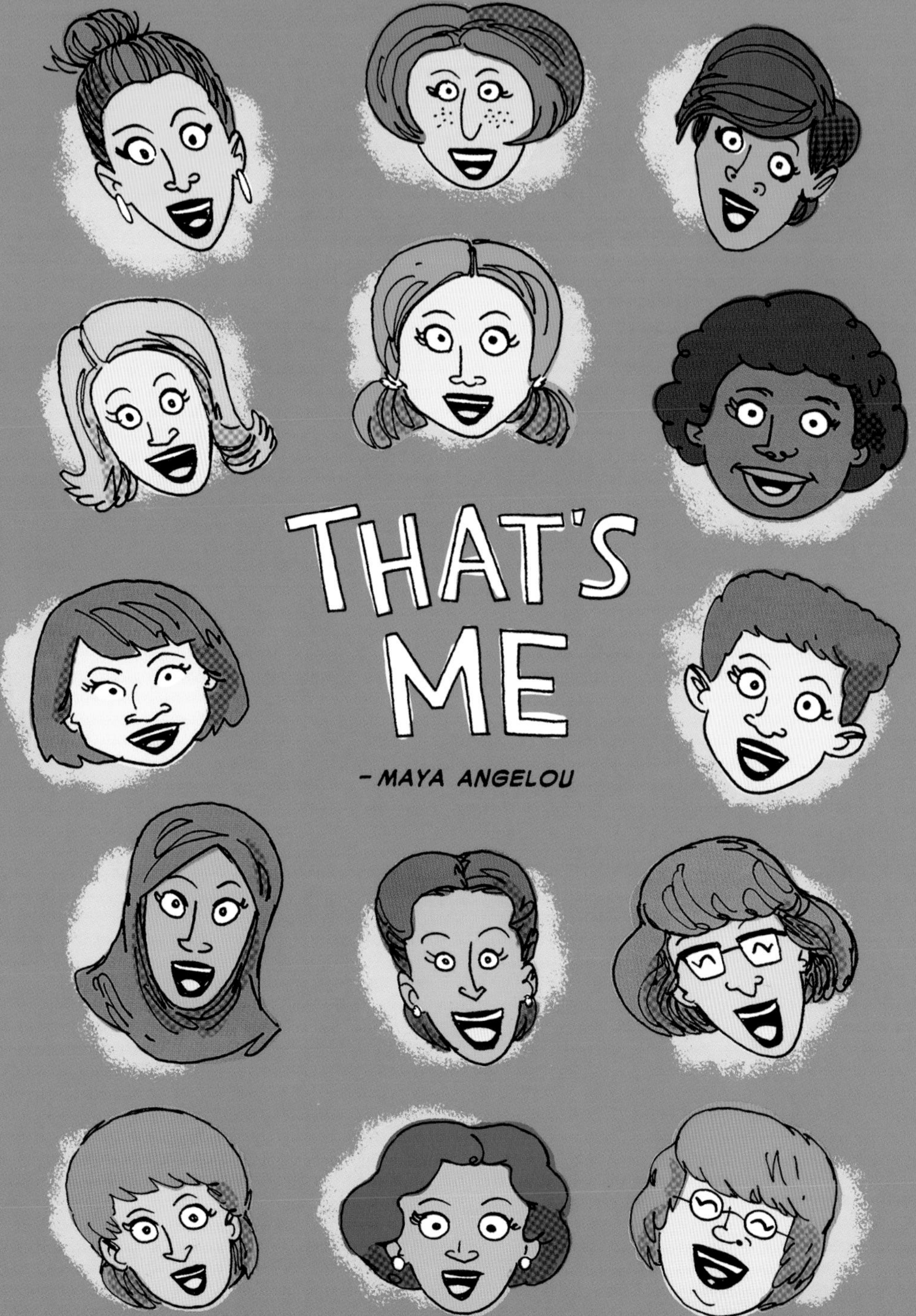
THAT'S ME
- MAYA ANGELOU

MARGARET E. KNIGHT

IT IS ONLY FOLLOWING OUT NATURE

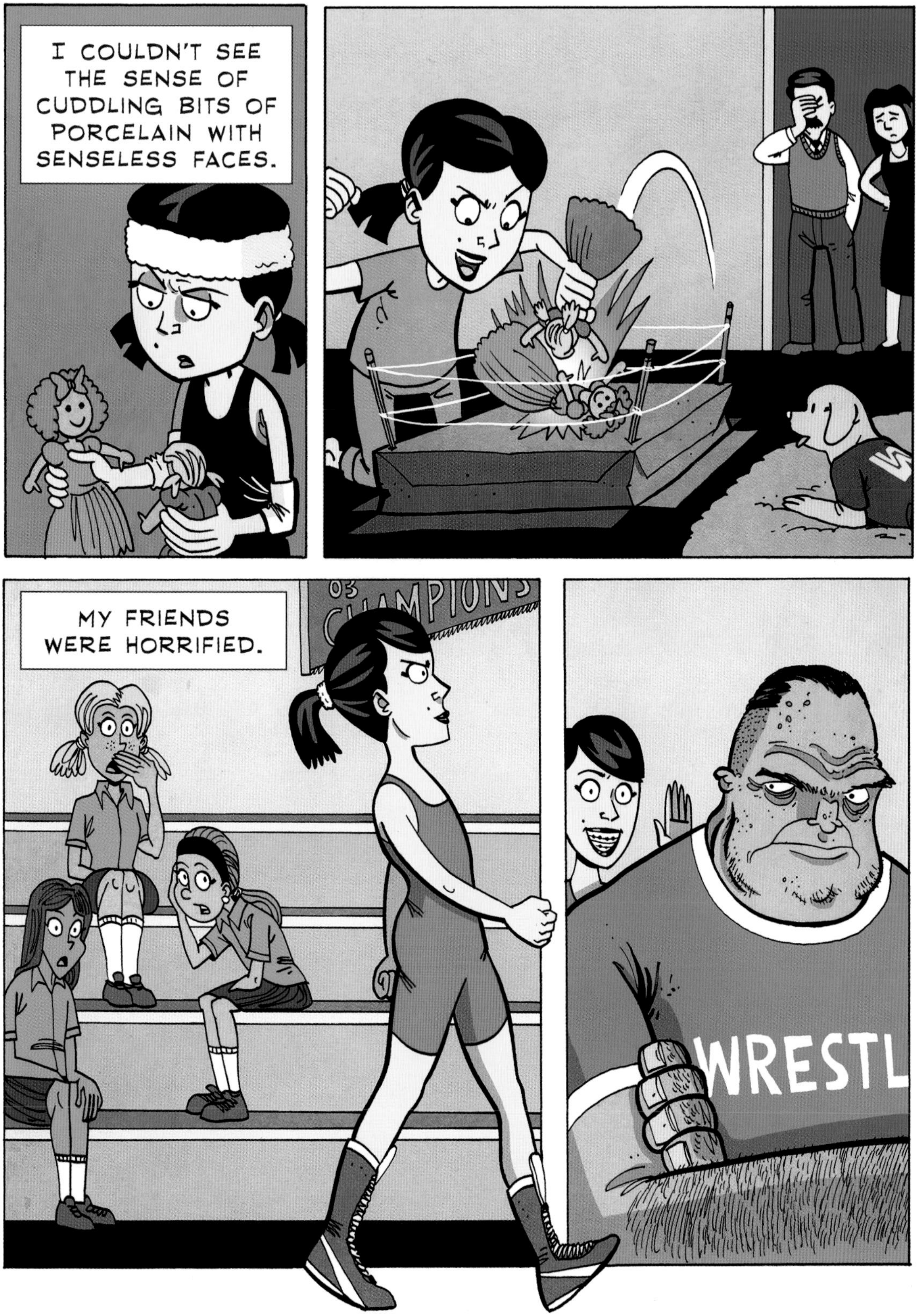

MY FRIENDS WERE HORRIFIED.

WRESTLING
BOYS
WRESTLING
TRYOUTS

BOYS
WRESTLING
TRYOUT

I WAS CALLED
A TOMBOY...

WRESTLING
...BUT THAT MADE
LITTLE IMPRESSION
ON ME.

I SIGHED SOMETIMES...
...BECAUSE I WAS NOT LIKE OTHER GIRLS.

BUT I WISELY CONCLUDED THAT I COULDN'T HELP IT...
IN THIS ISSUE
WRESTLIN
MONTHLY

...AND SOUGHT FURTHER CONSOLATION FROM MY TOOLS.
GYM

44lbs

RISE
RISE
RISE
RISE
RISING PHOENIX
RISE
RISE

Sports Illustrated

VS ANDREA THE GIANT

WRESTLING MONTHLY

I'M NOT SURPRISED AT WHAT I'VE DONE.

RISING PHOENIX
WRESTLING ACADEMY

Kahlil Gibran:

Work is love made visible.

And if you cannot work with love...

...but only with distaste, it is better that you should leave your work...

...and sit at the gate of the temple and take alms of those who work with joy.

For if you bake bread with indifference...

...you bake a bitter bread that feeds but half man's hunger.

And if you grudge the crushing of the grapes...

...your grudge distills a poison in the wine.

And if you sing though as angels, and love not the singing...

...you muffle man's ears to the voices of the day and the voices of the night.

– Kahlil Gibran

WILLIAM SHAKESPEARE

All the world's a stage...

And one man in his time plays many parts, **his acts being seven ages.**
At first the ***infant***, Mewling and puking in the nurse's arms.

Then, the whining ***school-boy*** with his satchel...

...and shining morning face...

...creeping like snail...
...unwillingly to school.

And then the *lover...*

...sighing like furnace, with a woeful ballad...

...made to his mistress' eyebrow.

Then, a *soldier...*

...full of strange oaths,
and bearded like the pard...

...jealous in honour...

...sudden, and
quick in quarrel...
...seeking the
bubble reputation...

...even in the
cannon's mouth.

And then, *the justice...*

...in fair round belly, with a good capon lined...

...with eyes severe...

...and beard of formal cut...

...full of wise saws, and modern instances...
SAVE OUR LAND
STOP FRACKING

...and so he plays his part.

The sixth age shifts into the lean and slippered ***pantaloon...***
...with spectacles on nose and pouch on side...

...his youthful hose, well saved, a world too wide...

...for his shrunk shank, and his big manly voice...

...turning again toward childish treble, pipes and whistles in his sound.

Last scene of all, that ends this strange eventful history...

Z z z
...is second childishness and *mere* *oblivion...*
Z z z

...sans teeth...

...sans eyes...

...sans taste...

...sans **everything.**
- *As You Like It*
Act II, Scene VII

JIM HENSON

A PUPPETEER'S ADVICE

OR HOW I LEARNED TO STOP WORRYING AND START ZEN PENCILS

THE DRAGONSLAYER
THE LOVER
BOY GENIUS

USUALLY ADOLESCENCE IS A TIME WHEN KIDS FEEL THAT THE WORLD IS DOING IT TO THEM.

DON'T HAVE A COW, MAN
COWABUNGA!
TURTLE POWER

WHETHER IT'S THEIR PARENTS DOING IT TO THEM...

HOMEWORK
HOMEWORK
HOMEWORK
HOMEWORK
HOMEWORK
HOMEWORK
HOMEWORK
HOMEWORK
HOMEWORK
HOMEWOR
HOMEWORK
HOMEWORK
HOMEWORK
HOMEWOR
HOMEWORK
HOMEWORK
HOMEWORK
HOMEWORK
HOMEWOR
HOMEWORK

...OR THEIR TEACHERS DOING IT TO THEM...
RELIGIOUS EDUCATION

SNIKT!

...OR THEIR OTHER FRIENDS DOING IT TO THEM...

...AND THAT THEY ARE THE VICTIM IN ALL OF THIS.
UNIVERSITY

SOMEWHERE IN HERE...

...YOU HAVE TO LEARN THAT YOU'RE NOT THE VICTIM.

ESCAPE PLAN:
· WEBCOMIC
· CARTOONS
· QUOTES
ZEN COMICS?
ZEN PENCILS?
SHAOLIN MONK
LOGO?
INSPIRATIONAL QUOTES
THE WRESTLER

THAT MOMENT IS SOMETIMES A LONG, SLOW REALIZATION...

...OR SOMETIMES IT'S TURNING ON A LIGHT SWITCH.

ALL OF A SUDDEN
YOU REALIZE THAT
YOU ARE THE PERSON
WHO HAS CONTROL
OF YOUR LIFE.
- JIM HENSON

THE MONSTER NAMED FEAR

BY GAVIN AUNG THAN

THERE'S THIS ONE GIRL WHO MAKES YOU LAUGH TILL YOU CRAMP.

AND ANOTHER WHO JUST WANTS TO BE *WORLD WRESTLING CHAMP!*

BUT THE ROAD TO THOSE DREAMS ARE FILLED WITH SOME DANGERS.
OBSTACLES IN THE WAY: PARENTS, TEACHERS, AND EVEN SOME STRANGERS.
MOST MEAN WELL BUT SOME ARE JUST MEAN...
...TROLLS SHOUTING AT YOU, THEY'RE DOWNRIGHT OBSCENE.
IT'S NEVER GONNA HAPPEN.
YOU'RE SO GONNA FAIL.
WHY DON'T YOU JUST QUIT?
IT'S EASIER TO BAIL.

NO! NO! NO!
THAT'S ALL THEY SCREAM.
YOU CAN'T DO THAT...
IT'S AN IMPOSSIBLE DREAM!

BUT THERE'S SOMETHING WORSE THAN THOSE DOUBTERS, YOU'LL FIND...
...KILLING MORE DREAMS THAN ALL OF THEM COMBINED.
IT WAS BROUGHT TO LIFE THE FIRST TIME YOU TRIED...
...I'M TALKING ABOUT THE MONSTER YOU HAVE GROWING INSIDE.
IT GETS BIGGER AND BIGGER, CRUSHING YOUR SOUL...
...UNTIL IT BREAKS FREE AND GOES OUT OF CONTROL.

YOUR ENEMY SPEAKS, ITS VOICE STRONG AND CLEAR:
HI, PLEASED TO MEET YOU.
MY NAME IS FEAR.

YOU SMELL A FOUL STENCH
AS IT GETS UP REAL CLOSE,
SCALY AND SLIMY AND
DISGUSTINGLY GROSS.
BUT YOU'RE NOT BOTHERED
BY ALL THE MUCUS AND GOO,
WHAT'S MOST DISTURBING IS THE
THING SOUNDS LIKE *YOU.*
I'M ALL OF YOUR FEARS AND ALL OF YOUR STRESS.
I'M YOUR FEAR OF THE SPOTLIGHT AND FEAR OF SUCCESS.
FEAR OF EMBARRASSMENT AND NOT ENOUGH TRAINING.

I'M WHAT SCARES YOU THE MOST...
...I'M THE FEAR OF YOU FAILING!
SOME SPEND THEIR WHOLE LIVES *RUNNING* FROM FEAR, EVEN WHEN THEY HAVE FRIENDS WHO SUPPORT THEM AND CHEER.

THEY GET GOBBLED UP AND DEVOURED BY THE BEAST...
CHOMP!
...THEIR DREAMS TURNED TO FOOD FOR THE MONSTER TO *FEAST.*
BUT DON'T WORRY TOO MUCH, HOPE IS NOT LOST...
PTOOIE!
...FEAR CAN BE BEATEN IF YOU'RE WILLING TO PAY THE COST.

THERE ARE STEPS TO TAKE, STEPS THAT ARE ESSENTIAL...

...TO MAKE SURE YOU DON'T LIVE YOUR LIFE ***NEVER REACHING POTENTIAL.***

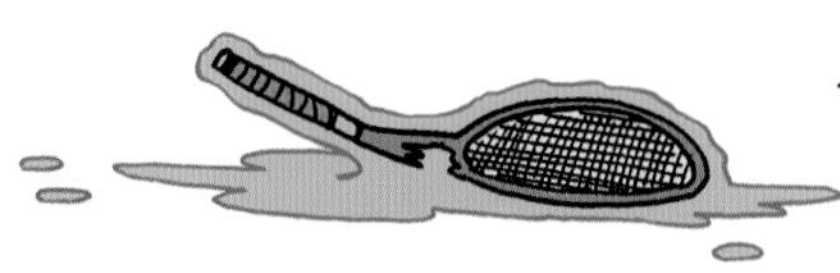

COMEDY PALACE

THOSE BUTTERFLIES ARE NORMAL YOU FEEL IN YOUR TUMMY...

...THAT'S WHEN YOU KNOW FEAR'S THERE...
...IN THE FRONT ROW...
...SITTING RIGHT NEXT TO MOMMY.

IT TAKES TIME TO GET BETTER, I KNOW PROGRESS IS SLOW...

...JUST ROLL UP YOUR SLEEVES AND KEEP *GIVING IT A GO.*

AND FOR THOSE SITTING AT HOME, THINKING THAT IT'S TOO LATE...

...FEAR CAN BE BEAT NO MATTER WHAT YOUR BIRTH DATE.
PAINTING FOR BEGINNERS
ENROLL TODAY

PRACTICE AND PRACTICE,
THEN PRACTICE SOME MORE,
AFTER SO MANY BATTLES
YOU'LL BE WINNING THE WAR.
SLOWLY BUT SURELY, YOU'VE
FACED FEAR HEAD ON...
...NOW THE BEAST IS NO MORE,
IT'S FINALLY GONE!

OOPS, SORRY...
I LIED, I MUST
TAKE THAT BACK...

...FEAR NEVER LEAVES, IT'S
ALWAYS WAITING
TO ATTACK.

IT'S LURKING
UP THERE,
INSIDE OF
YOUR HEAD...

...SOMETIMES IT COMES
BACK JUST WHEN YOU
THOUGHT IT WAS DEAD.

FEAR'S SCARY NO MORE,
NOT EVEN A ***FRIGHT,***
'COS YOU'VE PUT IN THE WORK
NIGHT AFTER NIGHT.

YEAR AFTER YEAR
AND THE END IS IN SIGHT,
NOW, AT LONG LAST
YOU'RE READY...

TIME TO FINISH THE FIGHT!

Isaac Asimov (1920–1992) was a writer, known for his contribution to science fiction and his staggering work in nonfiction and other genres. Asimov had a formal education in chemistry, teaching biochemistry at the Boston University of Medicine. He wrote and submitted fantasy stories in his spare time. He finally left the university in 1958 to focus on writing full-time. It seems to have worked out, as Asimov amazingly wrote over 500 books during his life. Asimov's nonfiction books were mostly on astronomy, but his titles also covered general science, history, mathematics, physics, Shakespeare, the Bible, and mythology. He was completely self-taught in these areas and successfully took difficult scientific concepts and made them entertaining for the general public.

Chris Hardwick is a stand-up comedian, podcaster, television host, and actor. The featured quote is taken from Hardwick's memoir *The Nerdist Way: How to Reach The Next Level (in Real Life)*. In the book, Hardwick shares how he levelled-up his own life and took control of his mind after years of excess in Hollywood. He went on to start the incredibly successful Nerdist empire.
www.nerdist.com

Sir Ken Robinson is a leading authority on education and creativity. A former professor of education, he now advises governments and businesses around the world and is one of the most sought-after speakers on education. He is also the bestselling author of *The Element: How Finding Your Passion Changes Everything* and its sequel, *Finding Your Element*. The words featured are taken from Robinson's famous TED Talk, "How Schools Kill Creativity." It is one of the most-viewed TED Talks ever . . . and also one of the funniest.
www.sirkenrobinson.com

Kevin Smith is a filmmaker, writer, podcaster, and professional babbler. Smith was twenty-four when his first film, *Clerks*, was released. He funded the movie himself for $27,000, using many of his friends as actors and filming it at the convenience store where he worked. The film was screened at the Sundance Film Festival, won the Filmmaker's Trophy, and was bought by Miramax studios. It launched Smith's career and helped influence the indie film boom of the 1990s. The quote featured is taken from Smith's memoir *Tough Sh*t: Life Advice from a Fat, Lazy Slob Who Did Good*.
www.smodcast.com

Amy Poehler is a comedic actress, best known for her portrayal of Leslie Knope in the television show *Parks and Recreation*. She's also a former *Saturday Night Live* cast member and co-founder of the influential improv school The Upright Citizens Brigade Theatre. Besides being an incredibly talented and hilarious performer, Poehler has started projects to promote women's rights and empower young girls. Her website *Amy Poehler's Smart Girls* is a hub for young women to learn together and be part of a community.
www.amysmartgirls.com

Albert Camus (1913–1960) was an Algerian-French Nobel prize-winning author, whose best known works include *The Stranger*, *The Rebel*, and *The Myth of Sisyphus*. Before concentrating on writing essays, novels, and plays, Camus worked as a journalist and also joined the French Resistance during World War II, where he edited an underground newspaper. The featured quote is taken from Camus's essay "Return to Tipasa." The essay, written in 1952, is about Camus's journey from war-torn Paris, then to Algiers, and finally to the small town of Tipasa, where he had spent the best days of his youth. There, he reconnects with the beauty and light of life that he feels he has lost during years of war in Europe. Not only does he rediscover the joy and hope he believes one must live with, he realizes that he had it within him all along.

George Mallory (1886-1924) was an English mountaineer and possibly the first man to reach the summit of Everest, almost thirty years before Edmund Hillary and Tenzing Norgay. During a 1924 expedition, Mallory and fellow climber Andrew Irvine were last seen 245 meters from the summit before vanishing. Ending in what was the greatest mystery in climbing for over seventy-five years, Mallory's body was only discovered in 1999. It's still debated whether or not Mallory and Irvine reached the summit before their deaths. Mallory's most famous quote is the reply he gave when someone asked him, "Why do you want to climb Mount Everest?" Mallory answered, "Because it's there."

Tenzin Gyatso, The 14th Dalai Lama, is a Buddhist monk and the spiritual leader of Tibet. After being forced to flee Tibet in 1959 when hostilities with China broke out, he has lived his life in exile and has spread a message of peace and compassion throughout the world for over fifty years. The featured quote is taken from the Dalai Lama's Nobel Peace Prize acceptance speech in 1989.
www.dalailama.com

Amelia Earhart (1897- disappeared 1937) was a pioneering aviator. She was the first woman to fly solo across the Atlantic, first to fly across the Pacific from Honolulu to Oakland, and also set numerous altitude and speed records. A celebrity of her day, Earhart endorsed products, had clothing lines named after her, edited *Cosmopolitan* magazine, helped popularize flying to the masses, and was a hero to millions. On June 1, 1937, Earhart set off to be the first woman to fly around the world. After flying for over a month and with only 7,000 miles left of the journey, Earhart's plane disappeared in the Pacific Ocean. Despite the attempts of the most expensive naval search in history at the time, no trace of Earhart's plane was ever found.
www.ameliaearhart.com

Robert F. Kennedy (1925-1968) was an American politician. As attorney general, Kennedy laid the smackdown on organized crime, spoke out for civil rights, and was chief counsel to his brother, President John F. Kennedy. After his brother was assassinated, Robert Kennedy served as New York senator before running as a presidential candidate for the 1968 election. Committed to improving the conditions of the poor and racial minorities, Kennedy was the favorite to win the Democratic party nomination until he, too, was assassinated. The featured quote is taken from Kennedy's famous Day of Affirmation speech, given in South Africa in 1966. Kennedy's five-day visit to South Africa, where he spoke out against apartheid, inspired millions of South Africans. One of Kennedy's favorite quotes, which he used often in speeches, is by George Bernard Shaw: "There are those that look at things the way they are, and ask 'why?' I dream of things that never were, and ask 'why not?'"

Edgar Albert Guest (1881-1959) was a prolific and popular poet who wrote over 11,000 poems, was syndicated in over 300 newspapers, and had his own radio and TV shows.

Percy Bysshe Shelley (1792-1822) was an English poet. "Ozymandias," Shelley's most famous poem, was the result of a friendly competition between him and fellow poet Horace Smith. The participants would choose a theme and have only fifteen minutes to finish the piece.

Maya Angelou (1928-2014) was a modern-day Renaissance woman—author, poet, activist, dancer, singer, director, and teacher. "Phenomenal Woman" is one of Angelou's most well-known poems, and the scenes featured in the comic are based on actual events in her life. When she was a girl, Angelou was sent to live in California after angering a white store clerk in Arkansas. In the 1950s, Angelou spent many years as a popular calypso dancer and changed her name from Marguerite Johnson

to Maya Angelou during that time to help draw crowds to her performances. While living in Ghana, Angelou befriended Malcolm X and later supported Martin Luther King Jr. and the NAACP during the civil rights struggle in the United States. She also called Nelson Mandela a friend, meeting him shortly after his release from prison. In 1993, Angelou recited her poem "On the Pulse of Morning" at Bill Clinton's inauguration.
www.mayaangelou.com

Margaret E. Knight (1833–1914) was an American inventor. From a young age, Knight had a gifted mechanical mind and loved to build gadgets. She created her most famous invention while working in a paper bag factory in 1868. After learning the bags needed to be glued together by hand, Knight invented a machine that could automatically make flat-bottomed paper bags, the kind still used today. Knight is known as the most famous female inventor of the nineteenth century and went on to hold eighty-seven patents in her name.

Kahlil Gibran (1883–1931) was a Lebanese poet and artist who is beloved by millions thanks to his famous book *The Prophet*. It is one of the most successful books of all time, having sold over 100 million copies, second only to the Bible in the United States. Written in 1923, the book is a collection of twenty-six poems delivered as sermons by a prophet who is leaving a city to return home. Before he leaves, the people of the city ask him to share his thoughts about life's big questions such as love, marriage, children, pain, and freedom. The featured quote is taken from the chapter on work.

William Shakespeare (1564–1616) was an English playwright and poet who is regarded as the greatest writer of the English language. "All the World's a Stage," one of Shakespeare's most well-known monologues, is taken from his play *As You Like It*. Spoken by the weary traveller Jacques, it is a melancholy speech about the passing of time and inevitably of death.

Jim Henson (1936–1990) was a puppeteer, storyteller, director, writer, artist, experimental filmmaker, and creative visionary responsible for many iconic television shows and films including *Sesame Street*, *The Muppet Show*, *Fraggle Rock*, *Muppet Babies*, *The Dark Crystal*, and *Labyrinth*. Henson used puppeteering, an art form that was seen as crude, childish, and primitive, to bring joy to millions. At the height of its popularity, *The Muppet Show* was the most-watched TV program in the world.
www.henson.com

ACKNOWLEDGMENTS

Isaac Asimov excerpt © The Estate of Isaac Asimov, All Rights Reserved.

Excerpt from THE NERDIST WAY by Chris Hardwick, copyright © 2011 by Fishladder, Inc. Used by permission of Berkley, an imprint of Penguin Publishing Group, a division of Penguin Random House LLC.

SIR KEN ROBINSON quotes taken from his 2006 TED Talk, HOW SCHOOLS KILL CREATIVITY. www.ted.com/talks/ken_robinson_says_schools_kill_creativity

Excerpt from TOUGH SH*T: LIFE ADVICE FROM A FAT, LAZY SLOB WHO DID GOOD by Kevin Smith © 2012. Published by Gotham Books, a member of Penguin Group (USA) Inc.

AMY POEHLER quotes taken from her ASK AMY YouTube series. Visit Amy Poehler's Smart Girls: www.amysmartgirls.com

Excerpt(s) from THE MYTH OF SISYPHUS by Albert Camus, translated by Justin O'Brien, translation copyright © 1955, copyright renewed 1983 by Alfred A. Knopf, a division of Penguin Random House LLC. Used by permission of Alfred A. Knopf, an imprint of the Knopf Doubleday Publishing Group, a division of Penguin Random House LLC. All rights reserved. Any third party use of this material, outside of this publication, is prohibited. Interested parties must apply directly to Penguin Random House LLC for permission.

PHENOMENAL WOMAN by Maya Angelou used with permission of Caged Bird Legacy LLC.

"On Work" from THE PROPHET by Kahlil Gibran, copyright © 1923 by Kahlil Gibran and renewed 1951 by Administrators C.T.A. of Kahlil Gibran Estate and Mary G. Gibran. Used by permission of Alfred A. Knopf, an imprint of the Knopf Doubleday Publishing Group, a division of Penguin Random House LLC. All rights reserved. Additional permission granted by the Gibran National Committee, Lebanon. Any third party use of this material, outside of this publication, is prohibited. Interested parties must apply directly to Penguin Random House LLC for permission.

Jim Henson excerpt used with permission of The Jim Henson Company.

Gavin Aung Than launched the *Zen Pencils* website in 2012, with the hopes of becoming a full-time cartoonist after a career in graphic design. It has since been featured by *The Washington Post*, *The Huffington Post*, *Slate*, *Buzzfeed*, *Gawker*, *Brain Pickings*, *Upworthy*, *Mashable* and was named one of the top 100 websites of 2013 by *PC Mag*. He lives in Melbourne, Australia.

WITH THANKS

To my wife, Jessica, for always believing in my impossible dream and for being my number one critic. To my parents, who probably spent the equivalent of a whole college tuition on all of the comic books they bought for me as a kid, and to the rest of my family and friends for their constant support. To my literary agent, Adriann, for helping secure the permissions needed for this book and to my publisher Andrews McMeel and editor Dorothy, for taking a chance on a web-cartoonist from the other side of the world.

To all of the remarkable people featured in this book, thank you for allowing me to adapt your words into these comic stories. Your quotes have not only enriched my life, but allowed me to express myself in a way I didn't think possible. I hope I've done your words justice.

And of course, to all of you, my readers who have supported my website and the books. Thank you for letting me do this. —Gav

---

For more cartoon quotes from inspirational folks visit www.zenpencils.com

Andrews McMeel Publishing, LLC
an Andrews McMeel Universal company
1130 Walnut Street, Kansas City, Missouri 64106

www.andrewsmcmeel.com

15 16 17 18 19 TEN 10 9 8 7 6 5 4 3 2 1

ISBN: 978-1-4494-7192-7
Library of Congress Control Number: 2015909559

ATTENTION: SCHOOLS AND BUSINESSES
